AF269867

CHICAGO BEARS
vs.
GREEN BAY PACKERS

RIVAL RUMBLE

ELLIOTT SMITH

Lerner Publications ◆ Minneapolis

Lerner Publications Company
An imprint of Lerner Publishing Group, Inc.
241 First Avenue North
Minneapolis, MN 55401 USA

For reading levels and more information, look up this title at www.lernerbooks.com.

Main body text set in Aptifer Sans LT Pro.
Typeface provided by Linotype AG.

Editor: Matt Doeden
Lerner team: Martha Kranes, Sue Marquis

Library of Congress Cataloging-in-Publication Data

Names: Smith, Elliott, 1976– author.
Title: Chicago Bears vs. Green Bay Packers : rival rumble / Elliott Smith.
Other titles: Chicago Bears versus Green Bay Packers
Description: Minneapolis, : Lerner Publications, 2026. | Series: Lerner sports. Sports team smackdown | Includes bibliographical references and index. | Audience: Ages 7–11 | Audience: Grades 4–6 | Summary: "The Chicago Bears and Green Bay Packers are two of the NFL's oldest teams. They have faced each other on the gridiron for more than 100 years. Learn their histories and then choose your favorite!"— Provided by publisher.
Identifiers: LCCN 2024044976 (print) | LCCN 2024044977 (ebook) | ISBN 9798765668627 (library binding) | ISBN 9798765683484 (paperback) | ISBN 9798765681534 (epub)
Subjects: LCSH: Chicago Bears (Football team)—History—Juvenile literature. | Green Bay Packers (Football team)—History—Juvenile literature. | Sports rivalries—United States—Juvenile literature.
Classification: LCC GV956.C5 S65 2026 (print) | LCC GV956.C5 (ebook) | DDC 796.332/640977311—dc23/eng/20240926

LC record available at https://lccn.loc.gov/2024044976
LC ebook record available at https://lccn.loc.gov/2024044977

Manufactured in the United States of America
2-1013195-53830-12/10/2025

TABLE OF CONTENTS

CLASSIC COMEBACK

The opening game of the 2018 season couldn't have started any better for the Chicago Bears. In the third quarter, they held a 20–0 lead over their rival, the Green Bay Packers. Packers star quarterback Aaron Rodgers was out of the game after hurting his knee. Everything was set up for a Chicago victory.

But the Packers had other plans. Rodgers surprised fans by returning to the field. He started firing footballs to open receivers. The Bears could not stop him. But there was still some hope. The Packers trailed 23–17 with about two minutes left in

Green Bay's Randall Cobb (right) sprints for a touchdown in the opening game of the 2018 season against the Bears.

the game. It looked like they would run out of time before they could steal the lead. Chicago's defense needed one last stop to finish the upset victory.

Rodgers dropped back to pass. He found wide receiver Randall Cobb over the middle of the field. Cobb caught the pass and sprinted to the end zone! The 75-yard touchdown pass gave Green Bay a dramatic 24–23 win. It was just the latest thrilling game in the long history between two of the oldest National Football League (NFL) teams.

FAST FACTS

- The Packers lead the all-time series against the Bears 107–95.
- Chicago has the most members in the Pro Football Hall of Fame with 34.
- The Super Bowl trophy is named after legendary Packers coach Vince Lombardi.
- From 1921 to 1970, the Bears played at baseball's Wrigley Field.

The Packers and Bears have a long history together. They have played each other more than two hundred times! The Packers lead the all-time series with 107 wins. The Bears have 95 wins, while six games have ended in a tie.

From 2011 to 2024, Green Bay won 24 of 28 games against Chicago. That recent dominance hasn't dulled the rivalry between these teams, which are only 208 miles (335 km) apart. For more than 100 years, the Bears and Packers have played a huge role in NFL history. But which team is the best? Let the rival rumble begin!

Running back Jordan Howard of the Bears carries the ball in a 2018 game against the Packers.

SMACKDOWN!

George Halas (left) with teammates in 1920

HISTORY OF SUCCESS

In the 1910s, professional football was just getting started. Many of the teams were in small Midwest towns. The Decatur Staleys were formed by the Staley Starch Company in Illinois in 1919. In 1920, they joined the American Professional Football Association (APFA) under coach George Halas.

In 1921, the Staleys moved to Chicago. A year later, the APFA became the NFL. The team played at Wrigley Field, home of the Chicago Cubs baseball team. In 1922, the Staleys changed their name to the Bears. The team was one of the best in the early NFL.

Chicago won eight NFL Championships before the first Super Bowl in 1967. Halas was the legendary coach of the team and later became its owner. His daughter, Virginia Halas McCaskey, still owns the team.

The Bears became known for their tough defense. They went 15–1 in the 1985 regular season. The team went on to win the Super Bowl that season.

Chicago running back Bill Osmanski carries the ball in the 1940 NFL Championship Game.

The Green Bay Packers were also sponsored by a local industry. Earl "Curly" Lambeau worked for Indian Packing, a meatpacking company located in Green Bay, Wisconsin. He organized a team to join the APFA in 1921. The Packers are the only community-owned sports team. More than 500,000 people own part of the team.

Even though Green Bay is smaller than other cities with NFL teams, its fans are some of the most passionate in the NFL. The waiting list for season tickets is more than 140,000 names long. The average wait is more than 30 years!

The Packers have won 13 championships, the most in the NFL. They became a dynasty in the 1960s. Green Bay won five NFL Championships and the first two Super Bowls. They returned to Super Bowl glory in the 1996 and 2010 seasons. Green Bay is often known as Titletown.

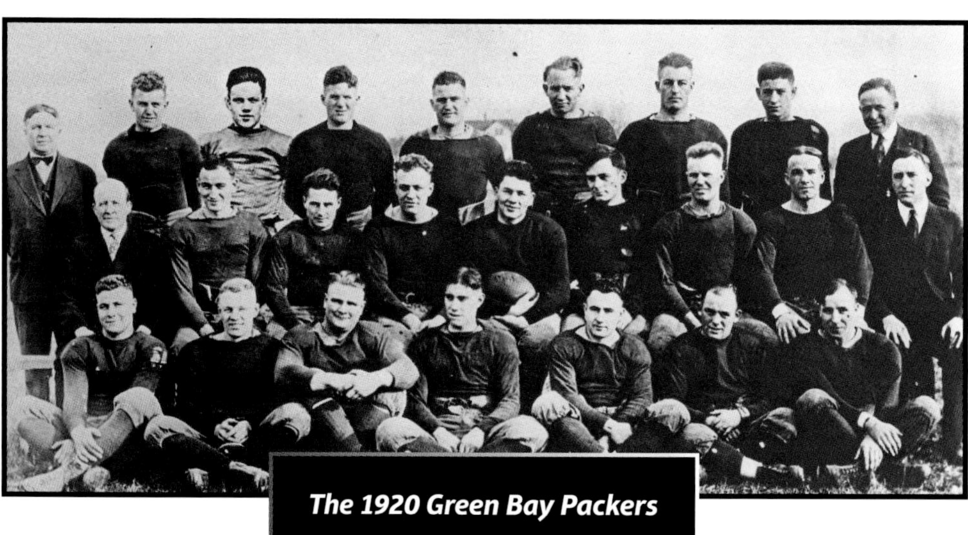

The 1920 Green Bay Packers

The Packers run a play in the 1968 Super Bowl against the Oakland Raiders.

After the 2024 season, the Packers led the NFL in all-time victories with 810. The Bears were second with 798. The two teams square off twice a season in the National Football Conference (NFC) North division. Their fans love watching their rivals lose almost as much as watching their own teams win.

CHECK IT OUT

The Packers' home stadium, Lambeau Field, is named after founder, player, and coach Earl "Curly" Lambeau. It is the second-largest stadium in the NFL.

CHAPTER 2

Green Bay running back Chuck Mercein carries the ball during the 1967 NFL Championship Game.

AMAZING ACHIEVEMENTS

Green Bay played in one of the most famous games in NFL history. The 1967 NFL Championship Game became known as the Ice Bowl because the temperature was –13°F (–25°C). The Packers trailed the Dallas Cowboys 17–14 with 16 seconds left and no time-outs. They were one yard from the end zone. Quarterback Bart Starr called a quarterback sneak and dove in for a touchdown to win Green Bay the title.

In 2000, the Packers and Vikings were tied in overtime.

Packers quarterback Brett Favre threw a long pass, but receiver Antonio Freeman slipped and fell. It looked like Minnesota would intercept the pass. But the ball went through the defender's hands and bounced off Freeman's helmet. Freeman snatched the ball out of the air inches from the ground. He got up and scampered to the end zone to give the Packers an overtime victory.

Antonio Freeman takes a big hit after making a catch against the Vikings in 2000.

Cornerback Al Harris scores a touchdown for the Packers after intercepting a Seattle Seahawks pass in overtime.

In the 2004 playoffs, the Packers and Seattle Seahawks went to overtime. Seattle won the coin toss and took the ball first. If they scored a touchdown, the game, and the Packers' season, would be over. But Packers cornerback Al Harris had other plans. He intercepted the Seattle quarterback and ran down the sideline for a 52-yard touchdown to give Green Bay the victory.

One of the greatest running backs in NFL history made his mark with the Bears. On October 7, 1984, Walter Payton became the league's all-time leading rusher when he finished a six-yard run against the Saints. The game was stopped as players from both teams celebrated the legendary running back. He ended his career with 16,726 rushing yards. The record stood for almost 20 years.

Running back Walter Payton flies over a group of New Orleans Saints defenders in 1984.

William "Refrigerator" Perry spikes the ball after scoring a touchdown in the Super Bowl on January 26, 1986.

Many players have scored in the Super Bowl. But none was like William "Refrigerator" Perry. In the 1985 season, the Bears used their huge defensive lineman to score touchdowns when they were close to the end zone. In the

CHECK IT OUT

"The Super Bowl Shuffle" was a song performed by members of the Chicago Bears that was released in December 1985. The Bears would go on to win the Super Bowl that season. The song was nominated for a Grammy Award!

Super Bowl that season, the Bears were rolling to victory and had the ball on the 1-yard line. Perry entered the game. He took the handoff and barreled into the end zone. Perry spiked the ball and became a hero in Chicago.

The Bears and Packers have had many memorable head-to-head games. On January 23, 2011, the teams met in the NFC Championship Game. It was the first time they'd faced off in the playoffs since 1940. A Green Bay interception sealed a 21–14 victory and a trip to the Super Bowl.

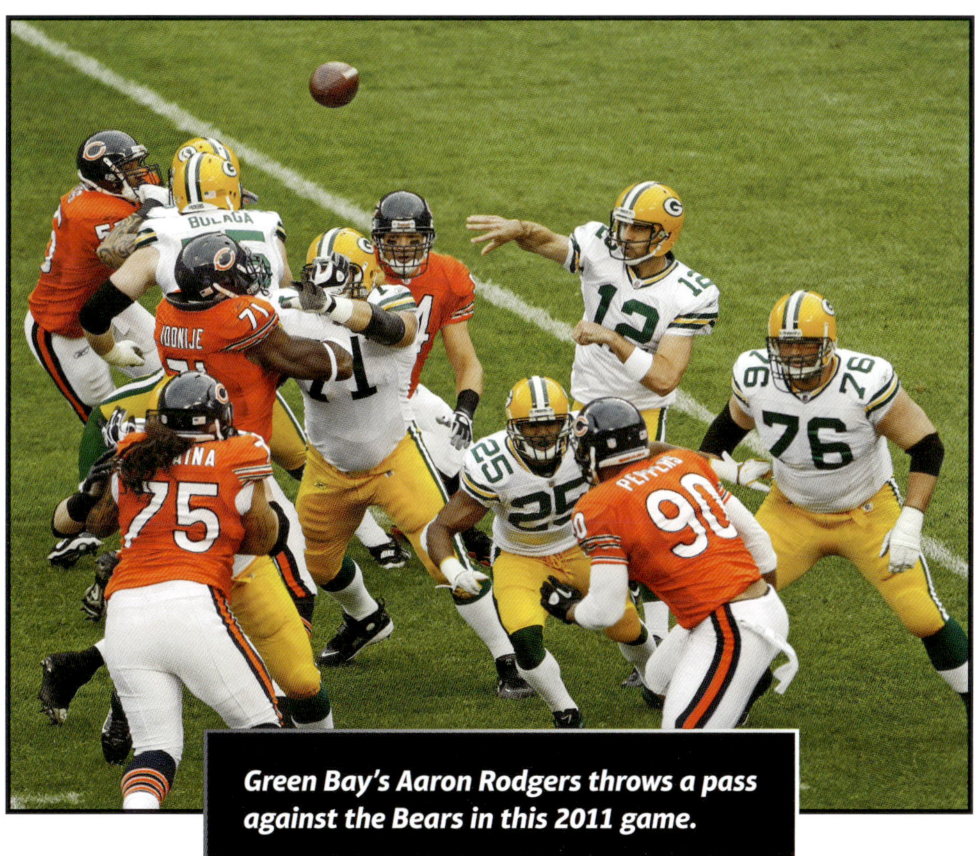

Green Bay's Aaron Rodgers throws a pass against the Bears in this 2011 game.

Green Bay defenders celebrate an interception in a 2022 game against the Bears.

In 2022, the teams met in a December game. Both teams had 786 all-time wins—tied for the most in NFL history. Green Bay claimed the top spot by themselves with a 28–19 victory. It was the first time since 1921 that the Bears had fewer all-time wins than the Packers.

CHAPTER 3

Sid Luckman is one of the greatest quarterbacks in Bears history.

LEGENDARY PLAYERS

The Bears have a long history of standout players and coaches. Chicago has the most members in the Hall of Fame with 34. From the league's earliest days, Bears players such as running backs Bronko Nagurski and Red Grange helped the NFL grow in popularity. Quarterback Sid Luckman won four championships for Chicago in the 1940s. He still owns several Bears quarterback records.

Linebackers have always been part of the Bears' success. Chicago's Hall of Famers at this position include Dick Butkus, Mike Singletary, and Brian Urlacher.

On offense, Mike Ditka was a star tight end for Chicago before becoming the team's head coach. Running back Gale Sayers is tied for an NFL record with six touchdowns in one game. Walter Payton remains second on the NFL all-time rushing yards list.

Modern Bears look to continue the team's winning ways. Young quarterback Caleb Williams has a strong arm and

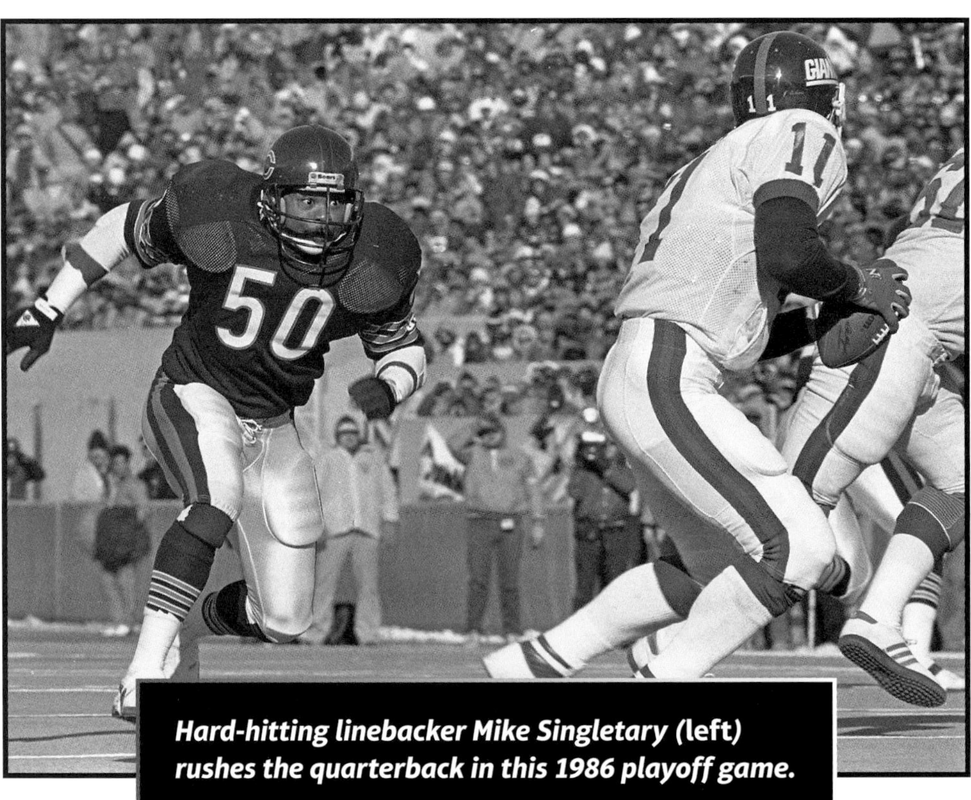

Hard-hitting linebacker Mike Singletary (left) rushes the quarterback in this 1986 playoff game.

Top: *Wide receiver DJ Moore runs with the ball.*
Bottom: *Quarterback Caleb Williams throws a pass.*

could be a star. Wide receiver DJ Moore is one of the best in the league at catching deep passes. And cornerback Jaylon Johnson is an All-Pro defender.

Green Bay has 28 members in the Hall of Fame. Coach Vince Lombardi won five championships with the Packers. The Super Bowl trophy is named after him.

Quarterback is a key position in Packers history. Bart Starr and Brett Favre are both in the Hall of Fame. Aaron Rodgers

Packers players carry coach Vince Lombardi off the field after winning the 1968 Super Bowl.

is sure to join them after he retires. Favre and Rodgers are fourth and fifth on the NFL's all-time touchdown passes list.

Defensive end Reggie White could wreck games for opposing offenses. He racked up 198 career sacks, second all-time. Cornerback Charles Woodson earned Defensive Player of the Year honors in 2009.

Reggie White (left) and Charles Woodson (right)

In the 2020s, Green Bay's team is full of stars. They include defenders Edgerrin Cooper and Kenny Clark. Quarterback Jordan Love hopes to lead the Packers back to the Super Bowl.

Quarterback Jordan Love looks down the field in a 2024 game against the Arizona Cardinals.

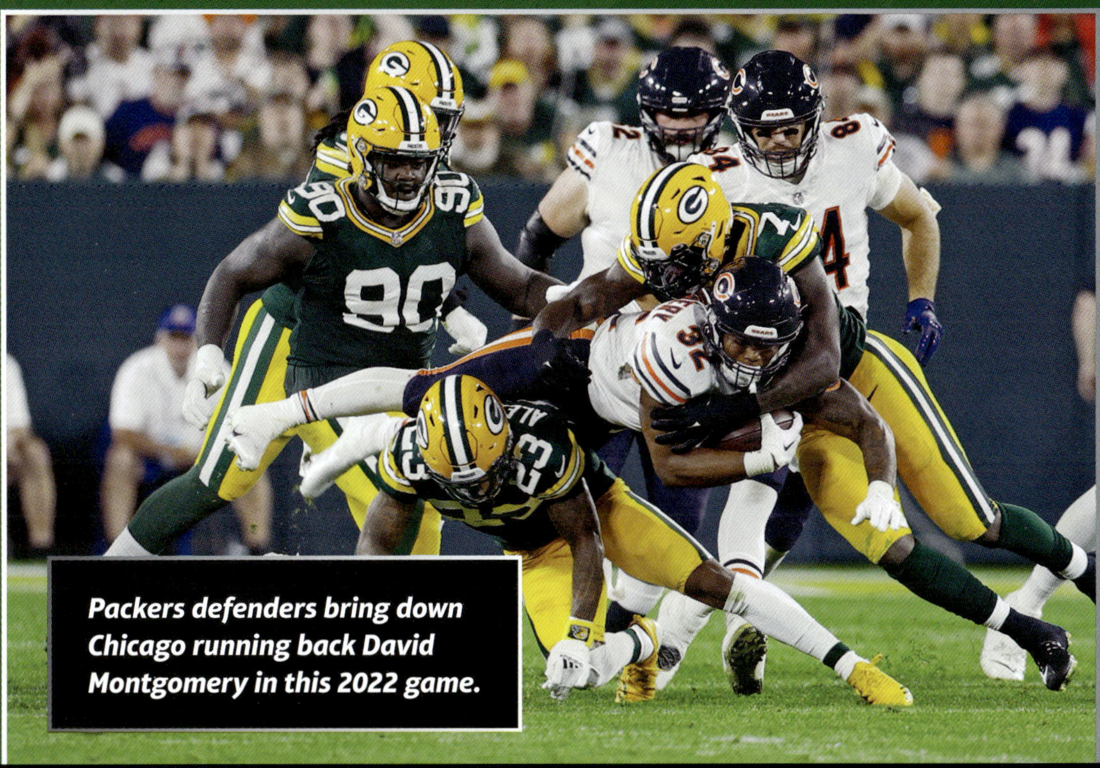

CHAPTER 4

Packers defenders bring down Chicago running back David Montgomery in this 2022 game.

CHOOSE YOUR CHAMPION

One of the best things about sports is that everyone can make their own choices. Comparing teams and debating which is the best is one of the fun parts about being a fan. There is no right or wrong answer!

The Packers have the most championships in NFL history. They are the only team owned by its fans. And Lambeau Field is one of the must-see stadiums in the league. The

Bears are the second-oldest team in the NFL. They have eight championships and the most Hall of Famers. The Bears have a young and exciting team ready to contend for the playoffs.

In this battle between NFC North rivals, the Packers have held the upper hand in recent years. The Bears have fielded

Chicago defender Khalil Mack (left) dashes down the field after intercepting a Green Bay pass in 2018.

Jordan Love hands the ball to running back Aaron Jones in the final game of the 2023 regular season.

some amazing teams, but they can't match the Packers' success. Therefore, the edge goes to Green Bay!

Now it's your turn. Who do you think wins this football smackdown?

SMACKDOWN TIMELINE

GREEN BAY PACKERS

1921 The Packers join the APFA, which becomes the NFL a year later.

1931 The Packers win their third straight NFL Championship.

1957 Lambeau Field opens. It is called City Stadium until 1964.

1967 The Packers reach the first Super Bowl, where they beat the Kansas City Chiefs.

1967 The Packers win the NFL Championship Game known as the Ice Bowl.

1996 Quarterback Brett Favre leads Green Bay to a Super Bowl title.

2010 The Packers win the Super Bowl with quarterback Aaron Rodgers.

2020 The Packers choose quarterback Jordan Love in the first round of the NFL Draft.

2024 In November, the Packers beat the Bears for the 11th time in a row.

CHICAGO BEARS

1919 The Decatur Staleys form in Decatur, Illinois.

1921 The Staleys move to Chicago.

1922 The team changes its name to the Chicago Bears.

1963 The Bears win their eighth NFL Championship.

1984 Running back Walter Payton becomes the NFL's all-time leading rusher.

1985 A strong defense leads the Bears to their first Super Bowl title.

2007 The Bears advance to the Super Bowl and lose to the Indianapolis Colts.

2024 The Bears draft quarterback Caleb Williams with the first pick in the NFL Draft.

2025 In January, the Bears beat the Packers to end Green Bay's 11-game winning streak.

GLOSSARY

cornerback: a defender whose main job is to prevent completed passes

division: a group of sports teams that often play against one another

dynasty: a team that has great success over several seasons

end zone: the area at each end of a football field where players score touchdowns

founder: a person who starts something new

industry: businesses that provide a product or service

interception: a pass caught by the defending team

linebacker: a defender who usually plays in the middle of the field

rivalry: fierce competition between two teams over a long period of time

title: championship

LEARN MORE

Bears Kids Club Central
https://www.chicagobears.com/fan-zone/kids-club-news

Green Bay Junior Power Pack Kids club
https://www.packers.com/fans/kids-club

History of American Football Facts for Kids
https://kids.kiddle.co/History_of_American_football

Leed, Percy. *Pro Football by the Numbers*. Minneapolis: Lerner Publications, 2025.

Rebman, Nick. *Green Bay Packers*. Mendota Heights, MN: North Star Editions, 2024.

Whiting, Jim. *The Story of the Chicago Bears*. Mankato, MN: Creative Education, 2024.

INDEX

PHOTO ACKNOWLEDGMENTS

AP Photo/Morry Gash, p. 4; Stacy Revere/Getty Images, p. 6; AP Photo/ Matt Ludtke, p. 7; AP Photo/Pro Football Hall of Fame, p. 8; AP Photo, p. 9; AP Photo/Pro Football Hall of Fame, p. 10; Focus On Sport/Getty Images, p. 11; Walter Iooss Jr./*Sports Illustrated*/Getty Images, p. 12; AP Photo/TOM OLMSCHEID, p. 13; Elsa/Getty Images, p. 14; Andy Hayt/*Sports Illustrated*/ Getty Images, p. 15; Focus on Sport/Getty Images, p. 16; AP Photo/Kiichiro Sato, p. 17; AP Photo/Nam Y. Huh, p. 18; Bettmann/Getty Images, p. 19; AP Photo/Paul Spinelli, p. 20; AP Photo/Mike Roemer, p. 21; AP Photo/Ross D. Franklin, p. 21; AP Photo, p. 22; AP Photo/Tom DiPace, p. 23; AP Photo/David Stluka, p. 23; AP Photo/Joe Robbins, p. 24; AP Photo/Darren Lee/CSM, p. 25; AP Photo/Jeffrey Phelps, p. 26; Cal Sport Media/Alamy, p. 27. Design elements: Trisno Wardana/Shutterstock; Ihor Biliavskyi/Shutterstock; Joko Ribowo/ Shutterstock.

Cover: AP Photo/Mike Roemer; AP Photo/Steve Luciano.